They called him the boy with the X-ray eyes...

France, 1940. World War II is raging. Times have been hard in Pierre's little village since the Germans took it over. For Pierre, things seem twice as hard, because he was born deaf and unable to speak.

But Pierre's eyesight is incredibly sharp. And one dark night, during a bombing raid, he sees a British plane go down in flames. Pierre can just make out the pilot's parachute, floating toward a nearby forest. The Germans will go after the pilot—and maybe kill him! Pierre has to find him first, and somehow get him back to safety. Can he do it? Or will he be captured himself?

Here is the incredible true story of a young boy's special courage in the face of wartime terror—a story so amazing you have to **Read It to Believe It!**

The Silent Hero

A true escape story from World War II

By George Shea

A Bullseye Nonfiction Book

Random House 🏠 New York

To Helene Mochedlover, of the Los Angeles
Public Library, and all librarians who care

Text copyright © 1994 by George Shea
All rights reserved under International and Pan-American Copyright Conventions.
Published in the United States by Random House, Inc., New York, and simultaneously in
Canada by Random House of Canada Limited, Toronto. Adapted from "Poor Pierre" by
Lore Cowan from the book *Children of the Resistance* (Leslie Frewin). Rights of *Children
of the Resistance* controlled by Leslie Frewin, England.

Library of Congress Cataloging-in-Publication Data
The silent hero / George Shea.
   p.   cm.—(A Bullseye nonfiction book)
"Read it to believe it".
SUMMARY: The true story of a young deaf French boy, Pierre, who rescues an Allied pilot
and helps him back across enemy lines during World War II.
ISBN 0-679-84361-2 (pbk.)—ISBN 0-679-94361-7 (lib. bdg.)
1. Pierre, 1926 or 7—Juvenile literature. 2. World War, 1939–1945—France—Juvenile
literature. 3. Children—France—Biography—Juvenile literature. [1. Pierre, 1926 or 7.
2. World War, 1939–1945—France. 3. Deaf. 4. Physically handicapped.] I. Title.
D810.C4S43 1994 940.53'44'092—dc20 [B] 93-5492

Manufactured in the United States of America 1 2 3 4 5 6 7 8 9 10

READ IT TO BELIEVE IT! is a trademark of Random House, Inc.

Contents

Chapter 1

The Boy with the X-ray Eyes

France. December 1940. No lights shined anywhere. Pierre could hardly remember a night so pitch-black.

He leaned out the window of his bedroom, straining for a glimpse of the nearby planes. He looked west to the Normandy shore, then north over the dark stretch of forest. But the clouds were thick and he could see nothing.

From the thin vibrations of the windowsill he

knew that only a few miles away, British planes were bombing and German guns were firing wildly back.

But he could hear none of this, not the planes nor the bombs nor the guns. Pierre was both deaf and mute. Since birth, he had never heard a word and had never spoken one.

Other children in the village made fun of him. They called him "Poor Pierre." They chased him and made up jokes and songs about him.

Nature had given him other gifts, though. He had wonderful sight—"X-ray eyes," his schoolteacher said—and an uncanny sense of direction.

As the old clock in the kitchen softly chimed the half hour, Pierre's great-aunt Marguerite came into the small bedroom. She was a tiny, wiry woman—tough, but devoted to her family and friends.

Marguerite listened to the sound of the planes and the shattering fire from the Germans. She pointed out the direction of the noise to Pierre. Together they watched that part of the sky closely. They had done this many times.

They had suffered over a half year of Germany's occupation of France. Germany was ruled by Adolf Hitler and the Nazis. They wanted to take over the world. Under Hitler, they had already conquered most of Europe.

Then, in the terrible spring of 1940, Germany invaded France, occupying its beautiful capital city of Paris. Now most of France was under Nazi control, including the three hundred people in Pierre's little village of St. Claire.

The Germans had chosen the countryside by St. Claire as a perfect place to build an airfield. It was near the coast, and near England, the country they were attacking now. The Nazi planes would not have to travel far over the English Channel to bomb England.

St. Claire had once been a lively and charming place. But the German occupation had robbed it of life. Farmers were ordered to give much of their produce—vegetables, fruit, cheese—to the Nazis. The soldiers patrolled the streets and kept a close eye on the villagers.

The days were grim, and the nights were worse. There was a strict curfew: everyone had to be in their houses by eight P.M. Anyone caught outside after eleven would be arrested, maybe shot.

There was nothing the people could do. But they fought back in their own way. Sometimes they gave the Nazis the worst produce, or served them bad food. They pretended not to understand the Germans' orders.

Marguerite hated the Germans more than most villagers. The Germans had killed all the men in her family, including Pierre's father. His mother had died when he was young.

As Marguerite and Pierre gazed at the dark

sky, the clouds suddenly broke. Searchlights weaved overhead, and in a split second Pierre saw a tiny flash streak across the sky. It could mean only one thing—a British plane had been hit! It was falling to earth in flames.

Then Pierre saw something else: a round white shape against the blackness. The pilot's parachute had opened! It was floating down toward the nearby woods.

It couldn't be far away, Pierre guessed. Perhaps a mile. He tugged on his aunt's sleeve and pointed to the sky.

Marguerite shook her head—she did not see the parachute. Pierre talked to her in sign language, his fingers moving rapidly through the air.

"Go," she signed back to him. "Go and find the pilot. Bring him here."

Pierre threw on his tattered wool jacket and his brown beret and headed out the door. He had to find the pilot fast. If the Germans had seen the parachute, they would send soldiers out. Their dogs would lead them right to the pilot.

Pierre jogged along the footpath that led through a meadow and toward the dark woods. He kept looking around as he ran. He would not be able to hear anyone sneaking up behind him.

His heart thudded in his chest as he sprinted in the dark. He knew what the Nazis would do if they caught him helping the pilot.

But he had one advantage over them. He knew the countryside here as well as he knew the flagstone path to his cottage gate. He knew each rise in the ground, and each dip that was slippery after rain. He recognized them at night as well as during the day.

Pierre was small, but strong and fast for his thirteen years. His sharp eyesight was invaluable to certain people in the village—people who worked secretly to destroy the Germans.

Some of the villagers had formed a network

of spies and underground fighters known as the Resistance. They were not trained soldiers but ordinary people—farmers and teachers, mothers and children. Pierre knew a few of them, but not all.

The Resistance leaders had sent Pierre out many times after curfew. He had a special knack for finding packages dropped by British planes. His eyesight was so good that even on the darkest night he could spot the shimmer of metal at thirty feet and see the clean line of a package resting high in the branches of a tree.

But this was not a package, or a message. This was a British pilot!

Pierre stopped in the shadows and searched the sky for the parachute. There it was, coming down over the woods! But what if the Germans got there first?

Up in the sky, pilot Jim Rush floated toward the

ground. When he looked down, he could see only blackness. He had no idea where he would land.

Rush was a lanky thirty-year-old American from Trenton, New Jersey. America was not in the war yet, but that didn't matter to him. Rush loved freedom and hated Hitler and the Nazis.

When Hitler began his attack on Europe, Rush went to England. He joined the RAF—the Royal Air Force.

That crisp December night, Rush's squadron of fighter planes had been sent to bomb the German airfield near Pierre's village. Rush was just turning back toward England when the clouds parted and revealed his position. A split second later his plane had been hit.

Rush had bailed out and pulled on the rip cord of his parachute. Seconds later, he heard the explosion as his plane crashed in the distance. He held his breath and prayed as his parachute drifted closer to the ground.

His fellow airmen had warned him about being shot down behind enemy lines. He did not want to imagine what might be waiting for him below.

Suddenly he hit something, and his legs gave out under him. He rolled on the ground and felt dirt and grass. He was lucky—he had landed in a clearing in the woods.

But his big white parachute stood out like a beacon. If the Germans spotted it, they would know exactly where he was. He had to bury the parachute!

Rush yanked off the parachute and pulled it toward him. Then he snatched up a tree branch and started to dig.

Off in the distance, he could hear the sound of an engine. A car or maybe a German truck. Suddenly he heard another sound. A crunch on dry leaves nearby. Something—or someone—was there, just a few feet away.

Was it a wild animal? A German soldier? It

was too dark to see. Rush dropped to the ground and pointed his gun toward the sound. He waited but heard nothing. Only the wind blowing through the trees. Only the sound of the car engine getting louder and louder.

He kept the gun ready, his heart pounding in his ears. Should he take a chance and run? Holding his breath, Rush pulled out his flashlight and clicked it on.

At first he saw nothing in the sudden glare. Then his heart froze. A small boy in a worn woolen jacket and beret stood at the edge of the clearing, silently watching him. Rush raised his gun and cocked the trigger

Chapter 2

The Secret Room

The wind blew loudly through the trees. Rush held his pistol steady. Who was this boy? A German informer? Should he wait to find out?

Suddenly the car engine stopped. Dogs barked, and men shouted in German. Rush had waited too long. The Germans were near!

He jumped up and spun around. There was nowhere to run, nowhere to hide.

Just then, the boy put his finger to his lips and stepped forward. He knelt down, pulled a jackknife from his pocket, and started slashing at the parachute. Rush watched for a moment, then bent down beside him. But he kept his gun ready.

For all Rush knew, the boy could be working for the Germans. He might try to win Rush's confidence and lead him into their hands. The Germans offered big rewards to villagers who helped them capture enemy fliers.

Together Rush and the boy cut up the parachute and buried it. The German voices and the snapping dogs were not so loud now. They seemed to be getting farther away.

"Who are you?" Rush whispered. But Pierre did not answer. Rush asked again, this time in French. Still the boy did not answer.

Pierre smoothed the earth over the buried parachute. Then he reached out and grabbed Rush's hand.

Rush had to trust him. There was nothing else he could do. He followed Pierre through the dark trees.

As they neared the woods, Pierre slowed down. Up ahead was the road into town. It was the fastest way to Pierre's cottage. It was also the most likely place to run into the Nazis.

Pierre tugged at Rush's sleeve and led him across the road. They crouched behind a hedge and peered out. Rush stared at the boy's face, twisted in concentration. "Who are you?" he said in French. "Where are you taking me?"

There was no response. Rush grabbed Pierre and shook him hard. "What are you doing here?" he demanded.

Suddenly an engine roared and a beam of light swept into the sky. Night turned into day. A car with a huge searchlight was coming their way!

They dropped to the ground and buried their faces in the dirt. The car stopped about fifty yards away, and two German soldiers jumped out.

"I swear I saw something crossing the road," one of the Germans said. "Here, run the light over those woods. See if we can spot anything."

The searchlight skimmed slowly toward Pierre and the pilot. They dared not move. As the beam swept above them and then away again, Rush let out a tiny sigh of relief.

The soldier raised his handgun, a Luger. "Come on," he said. "Let's have a look in this field."

Rush peered through the hedge. The Nazi was heading straight toward them!

"You're wasting your time," said the other German as he climbed back in the car. "Either he's dead or—"

"Shut up! Listen!"

"I don't hear anything. Let the others find him—if he's still alive. He won't get far."

A few moments later, with a screech of tires, the soldiers drove off.

Rush sat up slowly. So the boy was a friend after all. He had not given them away.

"Thank you," he said to Pierre in French, and took the boy's hand.

Pierre smiled, then led the way across the field. Rush had to follow closely. It was too dark to see clearly. But Pierre was fast and as sure-footed as a mountain goat. He made his way easily over the sloping fields.

At the edge of a tall row of pine trees, Pierre stopped. He put one finger on the glowing dial of the pilot's wristwatch, then held up two fingers and went off by himself in the dark.

What could the boy mean? Rush wondered. Two minutes? Two hours? Moments later Rush heard the sound of pebbles being thrown against a window.

Then he heard the creak of a door. In a flash Pierre was back. He led Rush to a little wood-shed and motioned him inside.

An old woman kneeled on the woodshed floor, a lantern beside her. She looked up as Pierre and Rush entered. "I am Marguerite," she said in English. She brushed a pile of dirt aside, then moved some heavy logs and a couple of wooden planks. A ladder led down into a hole in the ground.

"Come with me. We are friends."

Marguerite picked up the lantern and climbed down the steps. Pierre bolted the woodshed door, and he and the pilot followed her down.

At the bottom was a tiny basement room with dirt walls and a dirt floor. A cot sat against one wall, with a small table beside it.

Pierre had helped dig this room. He stared around at it now, hoping it was secret enough.

Marguerite lit a candle. "Do you speak French?" she asked the pilot.

"Not much," Rush answered. "But I understand a lot of it."

"Good," she replied. "You will be safe here. We will try to find a way to get you back to England. We are with the Resistance."

A huge grin spread across Rush's face. He knew all about the Resistance and the things they did. They rescued pilots like him who were shot down by the Nazis. They poured sand into the gas tanks of German trucks so the engines would not run. They smuggled secret information to the British.

And he knew that members of the Resistance were always in great danger. If they were caught, they were tortured and often killed.

Rush pointed to Pierre. "This boy—" he began.

"He is with the Resistance too," Marguerite said quickly. "He is my nephew, Pierre. He cannot speak or hear."

Rush felt terrible. He had been so angry with Pierre before.

"Can you tell him I am very sorry? I did not

understand," he said. "My name is Jim Rush. I am an American flying with the British. I am here because I want to fight the Nazis too."

Marguerite turned to Pierre and repeated the pilot's words in sign language.

An American! Pierre nodded to show he understood. He had never met an American before! Rush smiled and held out his hand. They shook, and then they laughed with relief at being safe.

"I am sure you are very hungry," Marguerite said to the pilot. She climbed the ladder slowly and went to the house for food.

Rush reached into his pocket and pulled out a square package wrapped in brown paper. He handed it to Pierre.

Pierre could not believe his eyes. It was a bar of chocolate! There had been very little candy in the village since spring. Even everyday foods like butter and meat were hard to find.

Pierre broke off a piece and offered it to the pilot. Rush smiled and shook his head. He wanted Pierre to have it all.

Pierre put the chocolate carefully in his mouth and licked the little smears from his fingers. He closed his eyes and chewed slowly. This was the most delicious food he had ever tasted.

When Marguerite came back with some bread and cheese, she laughed at the sight of Pierre so absorbed in the chocolate. "Thank you," she said to Rush, then turned to her nephew.

"Don't eat that all at once," she warned him in sign language. "And don't let anyone see it. They will want to know where you got it. In fact, I think you'd better leave it with me." She held out her hand.

Pierre took another tiny bite and gave her the chocolate.

Marguerite turned to the pilot. "Tomorrow we will make some plans," she said. "Tell me, what is your identity card number? The Resistance will need it."

Rush pulled out his identity card. All RAF pilots carried one. By the light of the candle, he read the number to Marguerite. "3-4-7-1."

"Good," said Marguerite. She repeated the number to Pierre in sign language. "It is important that you remember the number," she said to him. "My memory is not as good as it once was. You must remember this number. Repeat it to yourself until you do."

Pierre nodded.

Turning back to the pilot, Marguerite said, "And for now you must sleep." There was no heat in the dirt cellar, but there were thick wool blankets on the cot. Rush would be warm enough.

"Good night," Marguerite said to the pilot as she climbed the ladder.

Pierre raised his index and middle fingers to make a V. The V stood for "Victory." It was a symbol of the Resistance and their fight against the Germans.

Rush laughed and made the sign back.

Then Pierre climbed up the ladder. Carefully he replaced the planks and logs above the secret opening.

Back in the cottage kitchen, Marguerite put the chocolate in a drawer. Pierre repeated Rush's ID number to himself: "3-4-7-1, 3-4-7-1..."

"You did well tonight," Marguerite said to him. "You were very brave. Your father and mother would be proud of you.

"Now you go off to bed." She kissed him good night. "I am going to stay up and"—she winked— "iron some clothes."

Pierre knew what that meant. Marguerite didn't use her iron to press clothes. It wasn't even a real iron. It was hollow—and it held a secret radio inside.

The Nazis did not allow people to have short-wave radios. They didn't want the French to hear any news from the Allies—the countries that had joined together to fight the Germans. And they didn't want the French sending messages to the Allies about German troop movements.

So Marguerite waited until it was late at night. Then she took the radio out of the iron. Keeping the volume low, she tuned to the special broadcast from London.

"Tonight," the announcer's voice crackled, "the RAF bombed a German airfield in France. Many German planes were destroyed. Only one British plane was shot down..."

Upstairs, Pierre lay in the dark, worrying about the pilot. Had anyone seen them? Had they left any footprints in the soft ground? Not everyone in the village wanted to help the Resistance. Some, like the class bully Andre Moulet, were even friendly with the Nazis.

Pierre jumped up and went to the window. Was that a flicker of light in the distance? He peered into the darkness. No, just a family of foxes trotting single file into the woods.

Pierre climbed back into bed. It seemed that the Germans had called off their search for tonight. But at daybreak, Pierre knew, they would be out again with their dogs and trucks and guns.

Chapter 3

A Visit from the Enemy

The next morning dawned bright and cold. A frost lay over the meadow. Pierre woke early with a start.

What's wrong? he thought, glancing around his small room. Then he remembered—the American pilot, hidden in the secret cellar beneath the woodshed. Pierre dressed quickly and hurried downstairs.

Marguerite was busy in the kitchen, scrubbing the day's ration of potatoes. The iron was back in its place by the wood-burning stove. Could last night have been a dream?

But when Pierre sat down at the wood plank table, Marguerite turned to him.

"We must be very careful now," she signed. "We cannot do anything to make anyone suspicious."

Pierre nodded solemnly. It was no dream.

Slowly he chewed the hunk of French bread that was his breakfast, along with a steaming cup of tea. The bread was dry and the tea was stale and bitter. Pierre remembered the chocolate Rush had given him.

When his aunt left the room, he went to the drawer and took out the bar of chocolate. But before he could take just one bite, Marguerite came back. Quickly he slipped the bar into his pocket and went off to school.

I will not let anyone see it, he told himself. I

will just eat a little bit now, and then a bit more on the way home. He broke off a small piece and put it in his mouth.

As he walked along the country lane that led to the village, he silently repeated the pilot's identity number. "3-4-7-1, 3-4-7-1..." The last of the chocolate melted just as he reached the schoolyard.

Pierre's school was a run-down brick building. Bombs had ripped open one wall at the back. But the large room at the front was undamaged. The children who came here from the village and nearby farms fit easily in. They were all ages, but the schoolteacher, Mr. Croteau, managed to help every one of them, even Pierre.

Today the schoolyard was buzzing with excitement. As Pierre opened the heavy iron gate, he could tell that everyone was talking about the bombing raid. Some of the children were running in circles with their arms out, pretending they were airplanes.

Pierre looked around for the friendly Mr. Croteau, but the schoolteacher hadn't arrived yet.

Andre Moulet, the bully, spotted Pierre and chased after him. He held up a make-believe gun and fired at Pierre. "Rat-a-tat-tat!"

Pierre dodged and ran away. When he stopped and looked back, the other children were laughing at him.

Pierre decided to ignore them. He went and sat, as he often did, in a corner of the yard. If they knew, Pierre thought to himself, that I rescued a *real* pilot from a *British* plane, they would not make fun of me.

Without thinking, Pierre took the chocolate from his pocket and brought it up to his mouth. He was about to take a bite when he realized what he was doing.

Quickly, he stuffed the chocolate into his pocket. But it was too late.

Andre walked up, a big smile on his face.

"Hey, dummy," he said. "What have you got there?"

Pierre could not read lips and he could not tell what Andre had said. But he knew what the bully wanted. He gripped the chocolate tightly inside his pocket.

"That was a big piece of chocolate," said Andre. "What is a fool like you doing with chocolate?" He shoved his hand under Pierre's nose. "Give me a piece. Right now!"

Pierre was frightened. He couldn't let Andre or the other children see the chocolate. What if they found out who gave it to him?

Pierre jumped up and moved closer to the school doors. Andre followed him.

"Didn't you hear me, dummy?" Andre shouted. He tried to shove his hand inside Pierre's pocket, but Pierre pulled away and jammed the rest of the chocolate into his mouth.

The bully grabbed him and spun him around.

"Where's the chocolate?" he yelled. Pierre swallowed hard and held out his hands.

Andre went roughly through his pockets. "You ate it!" he said. Then he shoved Pierre hard, knocking him down. "You'll be sorry," he snarled as he walked away.

The other children stood and looked at Pierre. No one went to help him. They were all afraid of Andre.

As Pierre got to his feet, the children began lining up at the door. The bell must have rung, Pierre thought. It was time for class.

But something was wrong. Pierre could see worried looks on the faces of his classmates as they turned to each other on line.

Then he realized that Mr. Croteau had not arrived yet. Every day he came early to talk to his students in the yard. Where was he? Pierre wondered. Why hadn't he come?

Had the Gestapo taken him away? The

Gestapo was the Nazi secret police. They tortured people for information about Resistance activities. They hunted down anyone who was against the Nazis.

A few months ago, Pierre remembered, the Gestapo came in the middle of the night to the village police chief's house. The chief had bragged to some friends that he could kill the Nazi captain at the airfield.

That night, the Gestapo dragged him out of bed without warning. He was never seen again. And no one ever found out who told the Gestapo what he'd said. Pierre shuddered.

Just then, a tall, thin woman opened the school doors. She clapped her hands for order.

"Silence, children!" she shouted. "Line up properly so we may go into the classroom."

Pierre darted out from the line to get a better look at her. She flashed him an angry look. "You there!" she shouted. "Get in line!" Pierre shrank back into place.

"Mr. Croteau has been called away," the woman said. "My name is Madame Claudel. I am going to be your teacher today."

Where had this woman come from? Pierre wondered. Although she was dressed like local people, her haircut was unusual and modern.

"Now, let's go in," she ordered. Quickly, the children entered the classroom and sat at their desks.

"Open your Latin books at page thirty-three," Madame Claudel said. "We will begin with the verb *to be*."

Pierre followed as best he could, but it was difficult. Croteau knew sign language. He always told Pierre what to do. But Madame Claudel did not know Pierre. She had no idea that he was deaf. He hoped she wouldn't call on him.

A few minutes later, his classmates stopped reciting and turned around. Pierre followed their gaze out the window. A Gestapo car was pulling up outside! Just then, Croteau ran through the door. He was out of breath but smiling.

"Sorry I'm late, children," he said as he shut the door. He turned to the new teacher. "Thank you, Madame Claudel, for—"

Bang! The door flew open again. Three Gestapo men walked into the classroom. Now Pierre was terrified. This had never happened before!

"Rise, children," Croteau said grimly.

Pierre stood up with the others.

The Gestapo captain stepped forward. The other two stood on either side of the classroom door. Pierre had never seen any of them before. But he noticed Madame Claudel smile at the captain. Then she turned and strode through the door.

The captain looked slowly around the classroom. His eyes seemed to stop when they came to Pierre.

Chapter 4

Teacher? Or Spy?

Pierre fought the urge to turn and run. Had someone given him away? Could it be Madame Claudel? What did she know?

"Please be seated, children," the Nazi began. "I am Captain Reiner. Some of you were probably awakened last night by antiaircraft fire. Of course we destroyed most of the enemy planes and drove the others off.

"But we believe one airman may have parachuted down. We think he may be still alive. We have not found him. But we will..."

He glanced at Pierre.

"We are offering a reward to any boy or girl who can help us. Fifty thousand francs and a nice medal."

Fifty thousand francs! The children looked at each other, their eyes wide. That was more than many of their parents made in a year!

"A wonderful reward," said the captain with a twinkle in his eye. "Yes?"

A long silence followed. At the head of the room, Croteau coughed.

"Answer me when I ask a question," the officer said sharply.

"Yes, sir," muttered a few of the students.

"Now, does anyone have anything they would like to tell me?" Reiner said with a smile.

No one answered him. The captain stopped smiling.

"Perhaps I can help you to remember," he said. "A boy was seen going into the woods last night. Can anyone tell me who that boy was?"

Again, no one said a word.

"What is wrong with your students?" Reiner said to the teacher. "Why can't they remember?"

"Perhaps they have nothing to remember," Croteau answered.

"I am not so sure." The officer turned to the students. "Let's play a game. It is called Guess Who.

"Now, suppose you children had to guess which boy would have been out last night. And a good guess could be worth fifty thousand francs. Who would you guess?"

A hand shot up. It was Andre. "I would guess Pierre Carot."

A gasp of astonishment came from the class. Reiner walked over to Andre's desk.

"Oh? And why would you guess Pierre Carot?"

"Because he was eating chocolate this morning. There hasn't been any chocolate here in months. I wondered where he got it."

41

Pierre had no idea what they were saying. But he watched every head in the room turn toward him.

"And where do you suppose Pierre got the chocolate?" Reiner rapped on Andre's desk.

"From...the pilot who was shot down."

The Nazi captain walked slowly to the front of the classroom.

"Pierre!" he shouted. "Come up here!"

Pierre had not heard a word. But everyone in the room was staring at him. Croteau motioned him to the front.

It's over, Pierre thought as he rose from his chair. They must have found the American. He clenched his fists. He was going to reveal nothing to the Germans.

Croteau turned to the captain. "About Pierre...there is something you should know—"

"You will tell me nothing!" the captain exploded. "I will question the boy!" He peered down at Pierre. "What is your full name?"

Pierre stared at his feet, afraid to look the Nazi in the face.

"Answer me!"

"Please!" Croteau cried out. "The boy—"

"Quiet!" barked the Nazi. He turned back to Pierre. "I will ask you one more time, boy. What is your name?"

Still Pierre did not answer.

The captain raised his hand to slap Pierre.

Suddenly Gabrielle, the druggist's daughter, jumped up and shouted, "Please, sir—Pierre cannot hear or speak!"

The captain looked around at the children, who nodded agreement.

"Is this true?" he asked the teacher.

"Yes," Croteau answered curtly.

The captain frowned. "All right," he said impatiently, "then how do you communicate with him?"

"In sign language," Croteau answered. "I can show you."

"Ask him where he was last night."

Croteau turned to Pierre. But he did not repeat the captain's words. In rapid sign language he said, "Tell him you were asleep in bed last night. And it was *I* who gave you the chocolate."

The chocolate? Andre must have said something about it, Pierre realized. Why had he ever brought it!

Pierre signed this answer to the teacher, who turned and repeated it to Reiner. "The boy says he was home last night from the moment he came back from school."

"Ask him where he got the chocolate."

Croteau did so and Pierre began to sign back.

"Stop!" shouted the Nazi.

He handed a piece of chalk to Pierre. "Write it on the blackboard!"

Pierre went to the board and wrote, "Teacher gave it to me yesterday."

Reiner turned to Croteau. "But there is no

chocolate in the village," he said. "Your own student has said so. How do you suddenly have chocolate to give away?"

The teacher opened one of his desk drawers and took out a dusty piece of chocolate.

"I got this from you Germans. You are so generous. When the soldiers first came to the village, they gave away free chocolate. I saved some."

Reiner stared at the teacher for a moment. Finally he said, "Tell the boy to return to his desk."

Croteau signed this to Pierre, who gave a gasp of thanks. He was not to be taken away by the Gestapo—at least, not now. His legs trembled as he walked back to his seat.

After a minute of silence, the captain addressed the class again. "We Germans are very good to those who are loyal to us. But any boy or girl who disobeys knows what to expect. We have a special room at Gestapo headquarters where we deal with such bad children!

"Remember, if one of you were to help the enemy airman, we will be sure to find you out. Tell this to your parents, and tell them of the fifty thousand francs. Heil Hitler!"

The captain marched out of the classroom, the two officers behind him.

No one said a word until the roar of the Gestapo car had faded down the cobbled streets.

Then Gabrielle turned angrily to Andre. "How could you do that?" she cried.

In seconds, the whole class was yelling at Andre. Croteau held up his hands for silence. Then he turned to Andre. "Why did you accuse Pierre?"

Andre hung his head. "I was mad," he said. "I asked him for a bite of his chocolate and he wouldn't give it to me."

"So you decided to get even by turning him in

to the Gestapo?" The teacher shook his head. "He could have been killed!"

"I'm sorry," whispered Andre.

"I hope your classmates are kinder to you than the Gestapo would have been to Pierre," Croteau said. He turned away. "All right, children. Let's continue with our lessons."

When the school day ended and the children began to file out, Croteau pulled Pierre aside and quietly shut the door.

"Tell me exactly what happened last night," he said to Pierre.

Pierre could trust Croteau completely. He was not just the village teacher. Croteau was also the leader of the local Resistance.

Pierre told him how he had found the pilot and brought him home, and about the present of chocolate, and eating it before school.

"That was a dangerous slip," the teacher

warned him. "We have important work to do. Another mistake and we could all be killed."

Pierre nodded, shamefaced.

"When you joined the Resistance, you took an oath to do your best," the teacher reminded him.

"Please believe me," answered Pierre. "I will not make another mistake."

Croteau clasped the boy's hand in his. "I know you won't," he said. Then he told Pierre about the reward. "Fifty thousand francs would make just about anyone help the Nazis. You must be suspicious of everyone."

Pierre thought of the new teacher, Madame Claudel. He nodded.

"I will visit your house tonight," the teacher went on. "We must find a way to get the pilot back to England. Do you know his identity card number?"

Pierre began signing it when the door suddenly opened, and Madame Claudel stepped in. She was carrying a stack of papers.

"Excuse me, Mr. Croteau," she said with a smile. "I would like you to look at these tests."

"Of course," said Croteau. "You may go now, Pierre."

Pierre walked home in the dusk, worrying about Madame Claudel. Had she been spying on them? Did she understand sign language? And why had she suddenly shown up today of all days?

Chapter 5

Rats in the Woodshed!

That night Pierre stepped quietly out of the cottage with a package of cheese and a loaf of thick French bread.

He crept to the woodshed door and knocked three times, then twice. This was the signal to let the American know it was either him or his aunt Marguerite.

Inside the woodshed, he lit a candle and quietly removed the planks over the secret door. In the dim light, he could see Rush crouching down in the hole.

Pierre brought the food over, and the American eagerly took it. He ate quickly.

When he was finished, he smiled and took Pierre's hand. "Thank you," Rush signed awkwardly.

Pierre laughed. Marguerite must have shown him! He taught the pilot how to sign "Thank you" correctly.

Then Pierre took out a small, bent photograph. It showed a young man in a French army uniform, smiling and waving to the camera.

Jim Rush looked at the picture. He knew the man in the photo must have been Pierre's father. He handed it back to Pierre and reached for his own wallet. He brought out a small photo of a young brown-haired woman in a striped dress. She looked happy.

Pierre suddenly realized how lonely Rush

must be, in this damp cellar in the earth, with no one to talk to in his own language. He held out his hand to the American pilot, and they shook. Then he had to go. Rush waved good-bye as Pierre put the planks back across the hole.

Outside, a dim shape moved through the night, heading toward the house. Pierre's heart started to pound, but then he remembered. It was Croteau. The teacher had come, as he said he would. Pierre ran up and let him in.

Inside, Marguerite sat at the kitchen table. The secret iron radio was beside her.

"Listen!" she said. "General de Gaulle is speaking."

De Gaulle was the leader of the Free French, all the French people who were against the Nazis. As he spoke on the radio, Croteau relayed his words to Pierre.

"Frenchmen and Frenchwomen! The day is coming when France will be free again. Help the Resistance! Long live France!"

Marguerite clicked off the radio and put it back inside the iron.

"Long live France," said Croteau. He made the V for Victory sign. Pierre and Marguerite did the same.

"We must hurry with the letter," Croteau said. "It will be eight soon. They shot a man in the next village only last week for breaking the curfew."

"So? We can only die once," Pierre's aunt snorted. "But before I do, I want to take some Nazis with me!"

Marguerite handed a pen and some paper to the teacher. She dictated, and Croteau wrote in fast spidery ink on the sheet. Then he signed to Pierre, "Quickly. What is the pilot's identity card number?"

Pierre knew the number well. He had repeated it to himself a hundred times. "3471," he signed.

The teacher scribbled it down, then looked

up suddenly at the sound of a car outside.

Marguerite made a quick sign to Pierre. Someone was coming! Pierre leaped up and busied himself with a toy construction set.

A moment later came a heavy pounding on the door and two Gestapo men burst in. It was Captain Reiner and one of the lieutenants who had visited the classroom that morning.

Pierre froze. The paper sat in plain view. And the iron radio was right beside it.

"Madame Carot?" asked Reiner.

"Yes, that's me," answered Marguerite.

The captain pointed to Croteau. "You again, sir." he said. "You seem to be everywhere I go today."

"Madame Carot asked me to come here tonight," the teacher said calmly.

"And what harm is he doing?" Marguerite snapped. "He is writing a letter for me to my only goddaughter. I have no education, I cannot

write! It would take so long for him"—she pointed to Pierre—"to put signs onto paper. So the
schoolmaster—"

"Calm down, Madame," the officer said. "I
would like to see this letter."

Croteau picked up the letter and handed it to
him.

The captain read the gossipy note, then pointed to the top of the page.

"This number. What does it mean?"

"It is part of the address," Croteau answered,
a little too fast.

"Oh? What is the address?" the captain
asked Marguerite.

"My goddaughter lives at 3471 rue de Lion in
Paris."

The captain shrugged and went on reading:
"'Things have been good in the village since the
Germans came. They are being very kind to us.'"

He threw the letter onto the table. "You are a

very wise woman, Madame," he said coldly. Then he noticed the iron.

"What a strange looking iron this is." He began to fiddle with it. "How does it work?"

"It is…broken," said Marguerite.

Pierre played idly with the construction set, but his eyes were on the captain. One turn of that little knob on the top, and the front would slide off and reveal the radio!

Pierre glanced at a bread knife on the table. He saw Croteau looking at it too. Pierre knew he was thinking the same thing. Would either of them be able to use the knife? Could Pierre really kill another human being?

But the Nazi grew bored with the iron and turned to Marguerite. "We have come to inspect your house. I will explain later."

"Certainly," said Marguerite.

The lieutenant stayed in the kitchen as Marguerite took Reiner around the cottage. Pierre looked intently at Croteau and read the message in his eyes. The American pilot could *not* be handed over!

Pierre glanced back at the bread knife. He moved casually to the table, picked up the knife, and cut a slice of bread.

He thought of his great-aunt in Gestapo headquarters. Of what the Nazis might do to her if they found the pilot. At the first sign of trouble, he knew he would plunge the knife into the lieutenant's chest.

But then he saw Croteau shaking his head slowly. Pierre put down the knife. What was the schoolteacher thinking?

Marguerite and Reiner came back into the kitchen. "Thank you for showing me the house," the captain said.

He stopped and pointed out the dark window. "What is in the yard back there?"

"Nothing much," said Marguerite. She

glanced at Pierre. "Only a small woodshed."

"Come on," said the Nazi. "We must have a look." He started for the back door with Marguerite and the lieutenant.

Pierre looked wildly around to Croteau. The teacher nodded quickly and rose from the chair. Pierre picked up the bread knife and held it behind his back.

Marguerite strode to the shed and boldly swung open the door. She stepped aside to let the Germans in.

"Take a look," she said carelessly. "But watch out for the rats."

"Rats?" said Reiner.

"Yes, big gray ones," said Marguerite. "And plenty of them."

The lieutenant brought out his flashlight and ran it quickly around the shed. "I see nothing," he said.

Reiner shrugged, and turned back toward the cottage.

Quickly Pierre set the knife gently on the table.

"Now," said the captain when they were all back in the warm kitchen, "I will tell you the real reason we came here tonight. You are going to have a guest."

"What guest?" asked Marguerite.

"There are not enough rooms in town for our enlisted men. A German soldier is coming tomorrow to stay at your house."

Marguerite nodded. "Of course. I will have the spare room ready for him." She knew there was nothing she could do about it.

When the Germans had left, Marguerite turned to Croteau. "What are we going to do?"

"That German is being placed here to watch you," Croteau said. "It will not take him long to smell out the American. We must get the pilot out of here as quickly as possible."

"How?" Marguerite asked.

"We'll have to make our move tomorrow

night," said Croteau, "at choir practice. It's our only chance." He turned to Pierre. "You must be there," he signed.

Pierre gestured as if to say, "But I can't sing."

"It doesn't matter," signed the teacher. "I have something more important for you to do."

Chapter 6

The Message in the Capsule

The next morning the German soldier arrived. He was a short, thin man with mousy brown hair. He went straight to the spare room and slept soundly until Marguerite woke him for dinner.

As the three of them sat quietly at the kitchen table, Pierre could tell his aunt was angry about the German's presence. She was an excellent cook, but she had burned the porridge and served the sausages cold.

Later Pierre made his way to the inn for choir practice. The church choir met every Thursday. It was the one night the villagers were allowed out after curfew.

The Nazis let the choir meet in hopes that some villagers would then be willing to help them. But two Gestapo officers were always present, listening and watching.

As Pierre walked along, he went over the instructions Croteau had given him. In his mouth was a tiny metal capsule that held a message. The most important thing, Pierre thought with a smile, was not to swallow the capsule!

Just then, a truck rounded a corner up ahead and drove slowly toward the inn. It was the Gestapo radar truck making its nightly rounds. With its heavy-duty antenna on the roof, the Germans could pick up any nearby telegraph signals. They would know if anyone was sending a secret message to the Allies.

But the truck did not usually pass the inn so early. The Germans had changed their route. They must be suspicious!

Pierre raced to the inn to tell the school-teacher about the truck. But inside, Croteau was busy talking with some of the choir members. Across the room the two Gestapo men stood watching them.

"I need to talk to you," Pierre signed to Croteau.

The teacher smiled and stuck an empty glass into Pierre's hand. "Not now," he signed. "Wait for the signal. Do your best."

Pierre went to the kitchen. The innkeeper, a burly old woman, nodded to a tray of wine-glasses. She motioned Pierre to take the tray to the Gestapo men.

Pierre's thoughts flew as he carried the tray out to the main room. The radar truck took about two hours to make a round. It was seven-thirty now. The truck would be back around nine-thirty. If he didn't get the signal from Croteau before then, he would not go through with the plan. They could all be caught.

Suddenly he tripped and stumbled. The tray flew out of his hands. The glasses hit the floor and shattered, and dark red wine spread out from the shards.

Pierre looked up and saw the two Gestapo men laughing. One had stuck his foot in Pierre's way on purpose. The other Nazi was pointing at Pierre.

"What's the matter with you, dummy?" he said. "Can't you see where you are going?"

"Madame!" the first Nazi called.

The innkeeper ran over. "Yes, sir?"

"Look at the mess this blockhead made!"

The woman glared at Pierre. He ran to the kitchen and brought back a mop.

"The poor fool does not understand a thing,"

the woman said to the German. "He is just a deaf and dumb boy. No one knows what to do with him."

"Well, *I* do," said the Nazi. He held up a glass. "Have him bring us some sandwiches! And more wine!"

The innkeeper waved Pierre back to the kitchen.

"Get going!" the Nazi said. He kicked at Pierre with his foot.

Pierre flushed with anger. But he smiled tightly at the sneering men and marched off to the kitchen.

Pierre stared at his feet as the cook made their sandwiches. A cockroach crawled along the floor. When the cook's back was turned, he squashed the bug and stuck it in one of the sandwiches.

He took the drinks and sandwiches to the Gestapo men. One of them patted him on the head and handed him a small coin.

Pierre smiled and nodded, and went to wait on the choir members. He glanced nervously at Croteau. No sign.

From across the room, Pierre saw the taller Nazi—the one who tripped him—make a face and point at his sandwich. Pierre smiled slyly in triumph.

As the choir practiced their Christmas songs, the Gestapo men watched closely. Pierre knew they were studying every face, listening to every word, for any clue that might tell them who was hiding the pilot.

He glanced at the old grandfather clock near the kitchen. Eight-forty.

At eight-fifty one of the Gestapo officers caught his eye and pointed to his empty glass. Pierre hurried over with a fresh glass of wine, anxious not to miss Croteau's signal. Then he sat down again to wait. If there was no signal by nine—well, perhaps by nine-fifteen...

Just as Pierre was about to give up, he felt a tap on his shoulder. It was the innkeeper. She handed him a broom and pointed upstairs.

Pierre glanced at Croteau. The teacher was wiping his eyeglasses with his handkerchief. It was the signal Pierre had been waiting for.

He climbed the staircase, wanting to look back with each step and see if anyone was following him. But he knew better.

On the second floor were several rooms that were used as quarters for Nazi officers. Light streamed out from the crack beneath one of the doors. Pierre innocently swept the broom across the floor, past the door, and on down the hall.

At the end of the hallway was the door he had been told about. It seemed to be nailed shut. But Pierre found the secret latch, and the cleverly disguised door swung open. Behind it was the rickety staircase to the third floor.

Pierre stepped inside quickly and closed the

door behind him. It was pitch-black—even *he* could barely see a thing.

Gently he stuck his toe out to find the first step. There it was! Had he made a noise? He climbed the stairs softly, holding the broom carefully so it wouldn't clatter against the wall.

By the time he reached the third floor, his sharp eyesight had returned. Before him a narrow hallway ran to the other end of the building. The doors were boarded up. Huge cobwebs stretched from floor to ceiling.

Slowly he walked to the end of the hallway, where a small black trapdoor overhead led to the attic.

With the broom, he tapped the signal on the door—three taps, then two. The door opened a crack, then swung down.

A tiny basket was lowered on a string. Pierre took the steel capsule out of his mouth and put it in the basket. Then he jerked on the string. From above, a hand pulled the basket up into the attic and shut the door.

Pierre turned back toward the dark stairs. What time is it? he wondered. The radar truck would be by again soon. Would the telegraph operator upstairs have enough time?

Pierre re-entered the narrow stairway to the second floor. By now, he figured, the operator would be tapping out the radio code signals for 3-4-7-1. And way across the English Channel, another operator would be receiving them. Pierre prayed that the Gestapo was nowhere close.

By the time he got back downstairs, practice had ended. It was ten-fifteen, and nearly everyone had gone. Croteau stood alone near the door, waiting for Pierre.

His eyes searched Pierre's. Had everything gone all right? Pierre blinked once for "yes," and then they headed out into the dark, chilly night.

The Gestapo men were right behind them.

As they reached the end of the street, the radar truck veered around the corner. Its antenna was moving in a slow circle.

Pierre's heart jumped. If the radar hadn't already picked up the telegraph signals, it would now. He had to do something!

But what? He could run in front of the truck. It was a stupid thing to do, but the Germans thought he was a fool anyway.

Pierre turned to run. Then, for a split second, he looked up at the top floor of the inn. He couldn't believe what he saw.

Madame Claudel—the new teacher—was at the attic window! So she *was* a Gestapo officer. And she had caught the radio operator!

But no! Pierre looked closer. She was climbing *out* of the window. And she was clutching a small case, the right size for a radio telegraph. *Madame Claudel* was the telegraph operator!

Croteau gripped Pierre by the arm. Pierre tried to pull free, but the teacher held him tightly and marched him away.

Suddenly Croteau spun back around, and Pierre stared in shock at the scene before them. Gestapo men were firing at the roof of the inn! The slim figure of Madame Claudel stumbled, then ran across the slanted tiles and disappeared.

Croteau pulled Pierre and they ran from the inn. When they were several streets away, the teacher let go of Pierre's arm. He was very angry.

"Pierre, you cannot do such things! What if you had been caught! I don't know what you thought you were doing," he signed to Pierre. "But you were very foolish. If you went back to the inn, the Gestapo would have caught you for sure!"

"I wanted to stop the radar truck somehow," Pierre signed. "The telegraph operator—it was Madame Claudel, wasn't it?"

"Yes," said Croteau. "She was sent here to help us. She is with the Resistance in England. I only hope she got away. Pierre, you cannot do such things! What if you had been caught?"

Pierre thought for a moment. "Wouldn't it have been better," he signed, "for the Gestapo to catch a deaf boy who can't speak and knows so little about your work, than Madame Claudel, who knows so much?"

The schoolteacher was quiet. Then he signed, "Perhaps. You are a brave fighter, Pierre Carot."

He put his hand on Pierre's shoulder. They walked on down the winding village street in silence.

Chapter 7

Bully for Pierre!

School dragged by the next day. When classes were over, Croteau did not stop Pierre as he left with the other students.

Pierre walked home slowly, worrying about Madame Claudel. Was she still alive? Had the message gotten through to England?

Suddenly a bicycle came out of nowhere and sped toward him. He jumped out of the way.

The bicyclist circled and stopped in front of him. It was Gabrielle le Blanc, the druggist's daughter.

"I'm sorry," she said. "I was going too fast. Are you all right?"

Pierre could not read her lips. But he understood what she meant. He nodded yes.

She reached out and took his hand. As she did, she placed a slip of white paper in his palm. Then she turned and pedaled off.

Pierre looked down at the paper. It was a message from Gabrielle's father: "Your aunt's medicine is ready."

He knew what that meant. Le Blanc was a member of the Resistance.

Pierre went to the drugstore, where Le Blanc handed him a bottle of pills and another piece of paper.

Pierre looked around behind him. The drugstore was empty. He opened the paper and read, "Be ready to move 3471 Monday night at eleven. Use both pills."

Pierre smiled. The message had gotten

through! He shoved the paper and the pills in his pocket and left the store.

Outside, Andre and another boy, Marcel, were leaning against the store window.

"What do you have in your pocket *now,* dummy?" Andre asked. He held out his hand. "More chocolate? Come on. Don't you want to share it with us? We're your friends."

Marcel laughed.

Both boys were bigger than Pierre. He couldn't let them see the message. But he was always being pushed around.

Andre stepped closer, and suddenly Pierre gave him a shove that sent him reeling back. Pierre began to walk away, but Andre raised his arms and stormed toward him.

Pierre turned and pushed Andre again, as hard as he could.

Andre hit the ground with a thud. "Get him!" he spluttered to Marcel.

Marcel took a hesitant step toward Pierre, but stopped when Pierre raised his fists.

"I said get him!"

But Marcel turned and walked away. "Fight your own battles!" he yelled back at Andre.

As Andre got to his feet, Pierre took a step toward him, fists clenched. Andre walked quickly away. He yelled something back at Pierre over his shoulder. Pierre grinned. It was easy to yell things when you were running away.

Pierre rolled the message into a tiny ball and swallowed it. No one would ever find it now.

It was nearly dinnertime when he got back to the cottage. The German soldier sat in the living room, writing a letter. The delicious smell of Marguerite's hearty vegetable stew drifted from the kitchen.

"Be a good boy, Pierre," Marguerite signed. "Go and get some more wood for the fire."

This was part of their code, in case the German officer knew sign language. It meant it was time to take food to the American.

Marguerite handed Pierre a package of bread and apples. He stuffed it under his coat and went quickly out into the night.

At the woodshed, he looked around to make sure the German had not followed him. Then he gave the special knock and went inside.

In the dark shed Pierre lit a candle and opened the cellar entrance. Rush was happy to see him—and the food. He reached eagerly for the bread.

When Pierre came back to the kitchen, the German soldier was sitting at the table, a steaming plate of stew in front of him. He looked up at Pierre questioningly.

Pierre smiled and sat down. He tried to eat calmly as the German stared at him another moment.

"So, Madame Carot." The German turned to

Marguerite. "What do you grow here, for your food?"

"Apples. Some cabbages. Other vegetables."

The German nodded, but he continued to ask questions about Marguerite, and Pierre, and their lives.

Pierre's thoughts were racing. It was only Friday. How would they make it through this weekend to Monday night—the night they planned to move "3471"?

On Saturday, the German announced he would be away for much of the day. A German army truck picked him up late in the morning.

Pierre took some food to Rush as well as a deck of cards. Jim showed him a funny game that had the two of them slapping piles of cards and laughing.

Then Pierre took out a piece of paper and pencil. With a few words and some sketches he explained to Rush the plan for Monday's escape.

The German was back that evening for dinner. Afterward, Pierre brought out his construction set, and the soldier smiled. He told Marguerite that he had a son about Pierre's age, who had the same kind of set. The German sat down to help Pierre build a bridge over the threadbare rug.

Sunday went by slowly. The German stayed in the cottage, reading and talking to Marguerite. When it was time to take food to Rush, Marguerite signed for Pierre to get some firewood. The German watched her hand movements closely.

"What are you saying?" he asked.

"I want Pierre to get firewood," she replied with a smile.

But the soldier pointed to the stack of wood in the corner. There was still plenty left from yesterday.

"Oh! I thought we had used it all up." She told Pierre to stay.

Pierre tried not to look upset, but it was difficult. His friend would have to go hungry that night.

Monday finally arrived. The day was cold and windy, the gray sky filled with clouds. A storm was coming.

Pierre walked out to the shore twice to gaze at the sea. The Resistance would be coming across the water from England to pick up Jim Rush.

Would they be able to find their way in the storm? Would they come at all?

At five o'clock he went to the woodshed—Marguerite had made sure to use up all the wood in the house—and took Jim Rush one last meal.

Pierre could only stay a second. He pointed at Rush's watch and flashed the number eleven with his hands—ten fingers up, then one. Rush nodded. "V for Victory," he signed to Pierre. "V for Victory," Pierre signed back, and left.

By six it was dark. The kitchen clock ticked slowly as they ate dinner. Eleven o'clock was still five hours away.

"Will you stay in the house tonight?" Marguerite asked the German soldier .

"Yes," the soldier said. "Why do you ask?"

"Because we have a...surprise for you."

The German looked across the table at Pierre. "What kind of a surprise?"

"It is a gift," Marguerite said with a smile. "Pierre will bring it to you later."

By ten o'clock, the wind was howling at the door. Still the rainstorm had not come. But it was not far away. In the living room, Pierre played with the construction set while the soldier wrote a letter to his family. Finally Marguerite stood up and yawned.

"Time for bed," she announced. She kissed Pierre and wished the German soldier a good night. Then she went off to her room.

Pierre brought the construction set over to the soldier. When they'd finished the first building, a sort of castle, Pierre went to the kitchen. From a barrel hidden in the pantry, he poured homemade cider into a tin cup. The kitchen clock said a quarter past ten.

The German raised his eyebrows when Pierre returned with the dark, frothy cider. He sipped, then smiled broadly at Pierre.

"So this is the surprise! I have not had cider like this in a long, long time."

A little while later, Pierre went back to the kitchen and poured another cup of cider. This time, he took a piece of folded paper out of his pocket.

Marguerite had ground the two pills into powder. Pierre opened the paper and stirred the powder into the cider. He looked up at the clock. It was ten-thirty.

The German smiled when Pierre came back. An extra cup of cider! He was delighted.

Pierre smiled back at him, hoping he wouldn't taste the powder. The officer took a big gulp, then another one.

Soon he began to yawn. One of the little wooden blocks dropped out of his hand.

He yawned again, more deeply, and said in German, "What is the matter with me tonight, little Pierre? Why do I feel so tired?"

Pierre laughed and pretended to yawn back. The German laughed and took another gulp of the cider. Suddenly he fell across the table. The little wooden pieces scattered to the floor.

Marguerite came quickly out of her room. It was five minutes to eleven. The pills had worked just in time.

She poked the German to make sure he was really asleep. "Stay here, Pierre," she signed. "I will go and get the American."

Out in the shed, she lifted the planks and Rush climbed out of the hole. He put his arms around her.

"I will never forget you and Pierre," he said. "He is the bravest boy I have ever known. Tell him that. As long as I live, Pierre will be my friend. I must say good-bye to him."

"No!" Marguerite said. "There is no time."

But Rush was already outside and halfway to the cottage. Marguerite ran after him.

Pierre jumped with a start when Rush entered. Then he smiled, glad to say good-bye to his friend.

The kitchen clock began to strike eleven. "Hurry," said Marguerite, rushing into the room. "We must go!"

"I want to give you something, Pierre." Rush began to take off his wristwatch.

Pierre stared in amazement. He had never owned a watch. But he shook his head and pushed back the American's hand. He could not take the watch.

Marguerite spoke the words Pierre was thinking. "It's too dangerous. You must leave no sign."

"You're right, of course," Rush said. He shook Pierre's hand one last time. "I will never forget what you've done for me, Pierre."

"We must go," Marguerite said, and led the pilot outside. Then she returned to the cottage and stood at the window with Pierre.

Two Resistance fighters came out of the shadows, dressed in black like fishermen. One of them was Madame Claudel. They led Rush toward the beach.

There a small boat would be waiting. It would take them back across the sea to England.

As Pierre watched the dim shapes move into the darkness, one turned around to look back. It was Rush, his hand held high in the Victory sign. Then they were gone.

Marguerite gave Pierre a big hug. They looked over at the sleeping German, sprawled on the table. He was snoring loudly.

"Come on," she said. "Let's carry our guest off to bed. He has had his big surprise. He must never know what happened while he slept."

Chapter 8

The Future Belongs to Us

Pierre went out often over the next days to stand in the bitter wind and stare at the sea. Was Rush all right? Had he made it safely back to England?

Sooner or later, a message would come from the Resistance in England. It would let them know if the escape had worked—or not.

One morning, as the children sat in Croteau's classroom, Gabrielle raised her hand.

"Excuse me, Mr. Croteau," she began. "Last

night my father asked me if I could remember a line from a poem."

"What is the poem?" asked Croteau.

"It was about Napoleon," Gabrielle said. "The line begins: 'The future...' But I can't remember the rest of it."

Croteau smiled and said, "Is this the line you mean?" He went to the blackboard and wrote: "The future, the future, belongs to me."

"Yes, that's it," said Gabrielle. "Thank you."

"You're welcome," said Croteau. Then he smiled quickly at Pierre.

The line of poetry was a message from the Resistance, the one they had been waiting for. It meant that Jim Rush was safe in England!

After that, life went on much as before. Food was still scarce. The Germans still occupied the village. The soldier went on living at Pierre's house. Every night he and Pierre played with the construction set. But the soldier never wanted any more cider.

Pierre thought a lot about the American pilot. Except for the Resistance members, no one in the village knew what had happened.

But for Pierre, things would never be the same. He could still neither speak nor hear. But he was no longer "Poor Pierre." He had saved an American pilot. He was not afraid of Andre Moulet. And somehow, the other children knew he had changed.

When he walked into the schoolyard now, they did not make fun of him. One day, Andre Moulet began to bully one of the younger children. Pierre stepped in, and it was Andre who ran away.

Another day, Gabrielle sat down beside him. She showed him a book she was reading. Other children drifted over. One of them had a ball. He bounced it toward Pierre, and Pierre threw it back. After that, Pierre started to play with the other children.

Christmas drew closer, and the German soldier was sent back to headquarters. Pierre was almost sad to see him go. But not Marguerite. She wanted nothing to do with any German.

The night the German left, Marguerite took out her iron radio. She signed the news to Pierre.

German planes were bombing cities in the north of England. The destruction was terrible.

"Is Germany winning?" asked Pierre.

"Hitler is winning the war for now," she replied. "But in the end, I do not believe he can win. The world will not let such a madman take it over."

"Who will stop him?" Pierre asked.

"Good people...like you and me and Mr. Croteau...and the American pilot."

Pierre gave his aunt a hug.

Later that night, when Pierre was in bed, the whole house began to shake. He ran to the window. The British planes had come again!

It was a clear, crisp night, unlike the one that

had brought Rush. Pierre stood for a long time and watched the sudden flares and streaks rise and fall in the sky. He watched, as he had before, for any planes that might be hit.

But no pilots were shot down this night. When the raid was over and the planes turned back across the sea, Pierre slowly saluted.

Someday France will be free again.
The future, the future, belongs to us,

he said to himself and to his American friend in the sky.

About the Resistance

The Silent Hero is based on a true story. Between 1940 and 1944, Pierre and other people in the Resistance fought secretly against the Germans in France.

They put bombs anywhere they could. Sometimes they stuck them inside loaves of bread. When the bread was cut, it exploded.

Irons like Marguerite's were used to hide radios. Sometimes radios were hidden inside teapots or tin cans. One woman hid one inside her birdhouse. A man hid his inside his false teeth!

To help the German armies, the Germans took over French factories that made bombs and other weapons. Members of the Resistance got jobs in these factories so they could cause accidents and slow down the German war effort.

Sometimes they snuck in at night and put

bombs in the factories. When the bombs went off, all the other bombs in the factory blew up too.

Many members of the Resistance worked for the railroads. They blew up the trains and switched signs from "stop" to "go" so the trains would crash into each other or run off the track.

And they used a special grease that was supposed to make the engine parts work better. But it didn't. When it was put on the engines, it only wore them out. Many German trains were destroyed that way.

The Resistance worked closely with the British and later the Americans. The United States joined the war in December 1941, more than a year after the defeat of France.

In June 1944, Allied troops landed on the Normandy coast near Pierre's home. The Germans tried to drive them back into the sea, but they did not have enough tanks or troops. More German soldiers and weapons had to be put on trains and sent to northern France.

But the American and British air forces were ready for them. They bombed the roads and railroads that led into northern France. Allied soldiers were dropped by parachute into France. They blew up bridges and cut telephone lines and attacked German soldiers.

The Resistance played its part too. Many Resistance fighters lived in small bands in the woods. They came out and attacked German trains and soldiers. They blew up trains and caused accidents. They destroyed bridges and blocked roads. Resistance workers who ran the trains made sure they were very slow in getting to Normandy. Many trains were held up for days or weeks. The German trains could not get to Normandy in time to stop the Allies.

The Allies drove deep into France. They took Paris back from the Germans in August. Before long, the Germans were driven out of France. And by May 1945, Hitler was dead and the Nazis had been defeated.

Find Out More

The Commandos of World War II, by Hodding Carter (Landmark Books/Random House, 1966, 160 pages). The amazing deeds of the specially trained British "private army," whose surprise raids against Nazi strongholds prepared the way for the Allied invasion of France.

The Day Pearl Harbor Was Bombed: A Photo History of World War II, by George Sullivan (Scholastic, 1991, 96 pages). The story of World War II, from Hitler's rise to power to the dropping of the atomic bomb, illustrated with dozens of photos and newspaper headlines.

The Story of D-Day: June 6, 1944, by Bruce Bliven, Jr. (Landmark Books/Random House, 50th Anniversary Edition, 1994, 160 pages). The action-packed story of the day the Allies landed in Nazi-occupied France—and turned the tide of World War II—by a journalist who was in the invasion on that fateful day.

When you are older, you may want to read *Hitler,* by Albert Marrin (Viking, 1987, 156 pages), a riveting account of the man who rose from penniless tramp to power-hungry dictator and brought about World War II, changing history forever.